For those who still fight for the land… For those who lend their voice to the ones who can't speak.

— H.G. / B.D.H.

For my family, with love.
— N.D.

The Bee Mother

By Hetxw'ms Gyetxw (Brett D. Huson)
Illustrated by Natasha Donovan

HIGHWATER
PRESS

A New Queen

Winter's chill recedes, and the spring salmon return to the fishing holes. It is an exciting time for the Gitxsan as life returns to the lax yip, the territory, and soon the majagalee, flowers, will bloom.

March is the time of Wihlaxs, Black Bear's Walking Moon. Nox Ap, the bee mother, awakens from her winter slumber[1] along the realm[2] of Xsan, the River of Mists. Nox Ap seems to appear from the great beyond as the bumblebee queen crawls out of her warm hiding space.

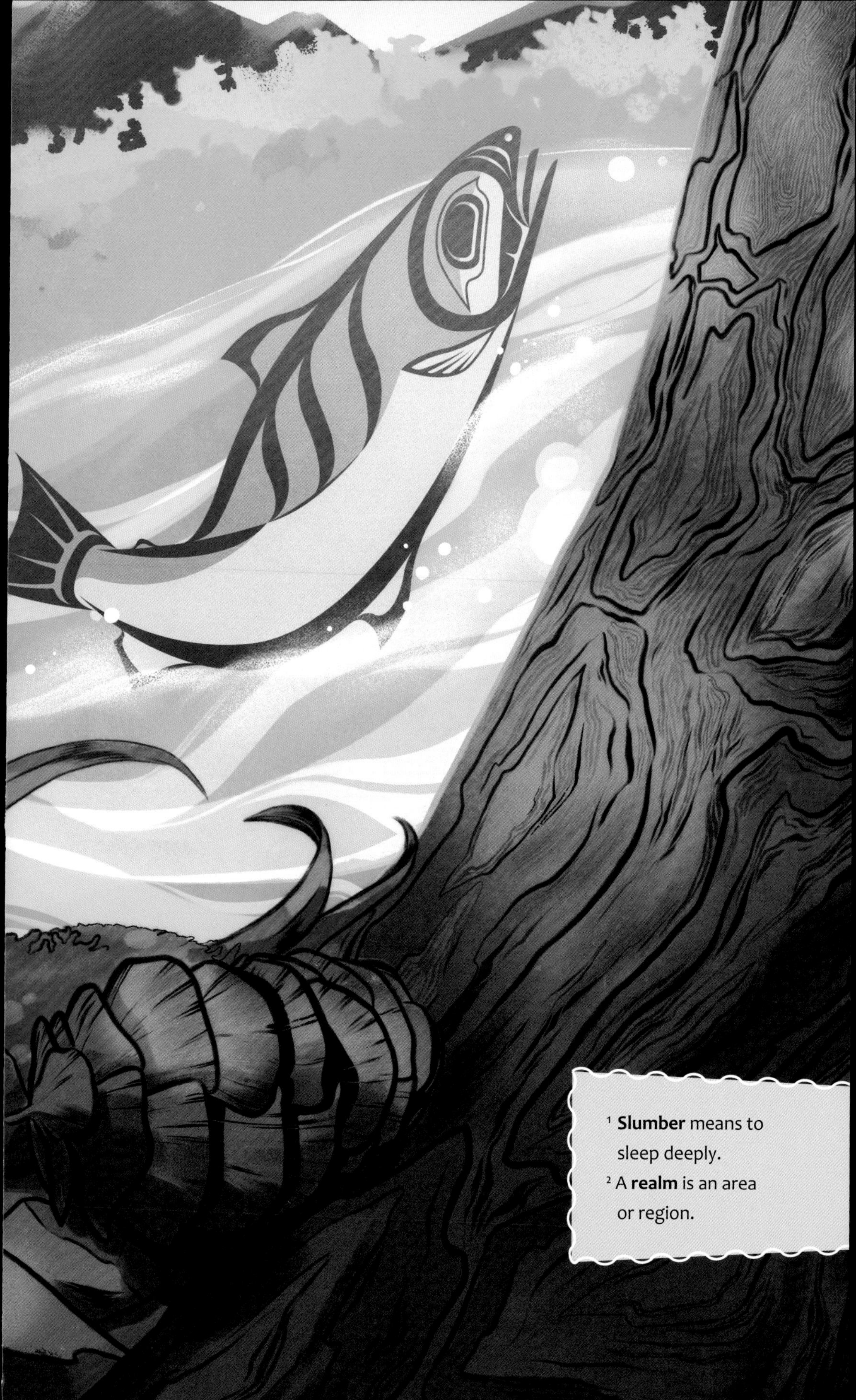

[1] **Slumber** means to sleep deeply.
[2] A **realm** is an area or region.

¹ A **burrow** is a hole or
    tunnel dug by a small
    animal or an insect.
² **Decaying** means rotting
    or decomposing.

Nox Ap is looking for a new home. She searches for a small underground burrow[1] or a hollow decaying[2] tree. Like Nox Ap, a yellow jacket wasp also seeks a new home. The yellow jacket queen needs space to hang her paper hive. Honeybees, more recently introduced to Gitxsan lands by settlers, have found their way into the wild. A swarm of honeybees and their queen have left an overcrowded hive to start a new one.

The yellow jackets build their a paper hive—called Anda Ap, bee pouch—on a sturdy tree branch, while the honeybees make a bigger home in the hollow of an old tree trunk. Although their homes look different, the process to build them is similar. They start by creating a series of small cells that will later make up the giant hive. The worker bees[1] will take over as the queen focuses on laying more eggs and growing the hive.

[1] **Worker bees** are female bees that build the hive and collect pollen and nectar to bring back to the hive.

Unlike wasps and honeybees, bumblebees don't build big hives, looking instead for places to build smaller nests. Nox Ap has found a place to lay her first eggs—in the hollow of a crumbling pine tree close to the pillowy moss floor. In her new nest she weaves her eggs in a cocoon[1] of food and wax. They will pupate[2] and eventually emerge from the cocoon as full-grown worker bees.

¹ A **cocoon** is a pouch or sack that protects insect pupae.

² To **pupate** means to grow from larva to an adult insect.

¹ **Pollinators** are animals or insects that move pollen between flowers.

A Busy Summer

It is now Lasa 'yan'tsa, the Budding Trees and Blooming Flowers Moon. After spending the better part of springtime building up her nest, Nox Ap will lay many eggs throughout the summer, including those that may become next year's queens. She sends worker bees out to collect the pollen and nectar needed to sustain the nest.

As pollinators,[1] bumblebees and honeybees are vital to the land. The people along the River of Mists know them as nature's gardeners, while their relatives, the yellow jackets, are nature's pest control. Though the yellow jackets are pollinators too, they are known for being predators, hunting among the flowers and plants for flies and other pests to bring back to their hives for food.

With the help of Nox Ap and her bee relatives, the fruits and vegetables that the Gitxsan depend on will thrive.

The honeybee hive has filled the hollow tree trunk and now oozes with honey. Unlike bumblebees, who store just enough nectar[1] to feed their queen through the winter, honeybees produce enough honey for the whole hive to survive with some left over to share. This honey is a new and welcome sweet food source for the Gitxsan. It is also a delectable treat for a lucky bear who happens upon a busy honeybee hive.

[1] **Nectar** is a sweet, syrupy substance that plants produce to attract bees and other pollinators.

Nox Ap's young queens and drones[1] are now flying out onto the land, leaving home for more solitary[2] living. Some will become food for birds, bats, and other insects. The solo drones have only one purpose—to mate with young queens who will start their own nests next spring.

[1] **Drones** are male bees. Bumblebee drones leave their nests as soon as they become adults.

[2] **Solitary** means alone.

³ A **nuisance** is a
    pest or something
    annoying.
⁴ **Integral** means
    necessary for
    completeness.

As the summer closes in on fall, the Gitxsan see more and more yellow jackets. This increase in wasps tends to occur when communities fill with the smoke of wilp sa hon, smokehouses. The yellow jackets can't turn down a tasty feast of salmon any more than a Gitxsan can.

More recently, people have come to see wasps as a nuisance.³ Still, their role in pollination and their voracious appetites for beetle grubs, flies, and other harmful pests are integral⁴ to healthy gardens and living spaces. But they're usually seen as unwelcome visitors as the Gitxsan prepare freshly caught salmon for the smokehouse.

Winter is Coming

Lasa xsin laaxw, the Catching-Lots-of-Trout Moon, cycles through Gitxsan skies. The cold October air means the season for pollination has passed. The bee mother is growing weary[1] and the young queens she birthed through the summer months have begun to settle into their winter hiding spaces.

Following the same cues,[2] the yellow jacket and honeybee queens have also found their desired overwintering spots. Like bumblebees, the survival of their species relies on the resiliency[3] of their queens.

¹ To be **weary** is to be very tired.
² A **cue** is a signal for action.
³ **Resiliency** is the ability to recover quickly.

[1] To be **invaluable** is to be too important to measure.

[2] **Abundant** means to have large quantities.

As many of the Gitxsan now fish for trout that are hungry and plentiful, Nox Ap is slowing down in her nest. The bee mother has contributed an invaluable[1] service to the land. The pollination her bees provided allowed food sources for all beings along Xsan to grow abundantly[2]—like the cherished huckleberries, strawberries, and soapberries used in many Gitxsan preserves.

When Lasa gwineekxw, the Getting-Used-to-Cold Moon, passes over, Nox Ap will succumb[1] to the cold. Her death is never an end. The spirit of Nox Ap lives on through Gitxsan stories and the hope her young queens will bring in the spring.

¹ To **succumb** is to die from injury or disease.

The Gitxsan

The Gitxsan Nation are Indigenous Peoples from their unceded territories of the Northwest Interior of British Columbia. These 35,000 square kilometres of land cradle the headwaters of Xsan, the River of Mists, also known by its colonial name, the Skeena River. The land defines who the Gitxsan are.

The Nation follows a matrilineal line, and all rights, privileges, names, and stories come from the mothers. Lax Seel (Frog), Lax Gibuu (Wolf), Lax Skiik (Eagle), and Gisghaast (Fireweed) are the four clans of the people. It is taboo to marry a fellow clan member, even when there are no blood ties.

The four clans are divided among the territories by way of the Wilp system. A Wilp, or house group, is a group comprising one or more families. Each Wilp has a Head Chief and Wing Chiefs, who are guided by Elders and members of their Wilp. Currently, there are 62 house groups, and each governs their portion of the Gitxsan Territories.

The Gitxsan Moons

K'uholxs	Stories and Feasting Moon	January
Lasa hu'mal	Cracking Cottonwood and Opening Trails Moon	February
Wihlaxs	Black Bear's Walking Moon	March
Lasa ya'a	Spring Salmon's Returning Home Moon	April
Lasa 'yan'tsa	Budding Trees and Blooming Flowers Moon	May
Lasa maa'y	Gathering and Preparing Berries Moon	June
Lasa 'wiihun	Fisherman's Moon	July
Lasa lik'i'nxsw	Grizzly Bear's Moon	August
Lasa gangwiikw	Groundhog Hunting Moon	September
Lasa xsin laaxw	Catching-Lots-of-Trout Moon	October
Lasa gwineekxw	Getting-Used-to-Cold Moon	November
Lasa 'wiigwineekxw or Lasa gunkw' ats	Severe Snowstorms and Sharp Cold Moon	December
Ax wa	Shaman's Moon	A blue moon, which is a second full moon in a single month

Stekyodin

Bulkley
River

Kispiox
River

Skeena River

Funded by the Government of Canada
Financé par le gouvernement du Canada

Canada Council for the Arts   Conseil des Arts du Canada

HighWater Press gratefully acknowledges the financial support of the Government of Canada and Canada Council for the Arts as well as the Province of Manitoba through the Department of Culture, Heritage, Tourism and Sport and the Manitoba Book Publishing Tax Credit for our publishing activities.

HighWater Press is an imprint of Portage & Main Press.
Printed and bound in Canada by Friesens
Design by Relish New Brand Experience
Cover Art by Natasha Donovan

Library and Archives Canada Cataloguing in Publication

Title: The bee mother / Hetxw'ms Gyetxw (Brett D. Huson) ; illustrated by Natasha Donovan.
Names: Huson, Brett D., author. | Donovan, Natasha, illustrator.
Series: Huson, Brett D. Mothers of Xsan ; 7.
Description: Series statement: Mothers of Xsan ; 7
Identifiers: Canadiana (print) 20240285654 | Canadiana (ebook) 20240285670 | ISBN 9781774920800
   (hardcover) | ISBN 9781774920817 (EPUB) | ISBN 9781774920824 (PDF)
Subjects: LCSH: Bees—British Columbia—Juvenile literature. | LCSH: Bees—Life cycles—Juvenile
   literature. | LCSH: Indigenous peoples—British Columbia—Juvenile literature. | LCGFT: Picture
   books.
Classification: LCC QL565.2 .H87 2024 | DDC j595.79/9—dc23

27 26 25 24   1 2 3 4 5

HIGHWATER PRESS

www.highwaterpress.com
Winnipeg, Manitoba
Treaty 1 Territory and homeland of the Métis Nation